ICONIC LONDON

ICONIC LONDON

Published by VisitBritain Publishing in association with Visit London

VisitBritain
Thames Tower, Blacks Road, London W6 9EL

Visit London
www.visitlondon.com

First published 2007

© British Tourist Authority (trading as VisitBritain) 2007

ISBN
978 0 7095 8417 9
Product code: IMAGES05

A CIP catalogue record for this book is available from the British Library.

The information contained in this publication has been published in good faith on the basis of information submitted to VisitBritain and is believed to be correct at time of going to press. Nevertheless, VisitBritain regrets that it cannot guarantee complete accuracy and all liability for loss, disappointment, negligence or other damages caused by reliance on the information contained in this publication, is hereby excluded.

The photographs in *Iconic London* were all chosen from VisitBritain's official online image library, Britain on View and include selected images from Visit London.

Editorial and design by Indigo 3 Publishing for VisitBritain Publishing.
Printed and bound in Dubai by Emirates Printing Press.

ICONIC LONDON

ICONIC  LONDON

Iconic *London* reveals the depth of history and the wealth of diversity found in one of the world's most cosmopolitan cities. It captures historic palaces, celebrated landmarks and famous museums, as well as the bustling streets and thriving culture that make London such a wonderfully historic, yet modern, metropolis.

From the excitement of the West End to the tranquility
of Hyde Park, from the splendour of Buckingham Palace
to the wonder of the 'Gherkin' and from the treasures
of the British Museum to the colourful spectacle of the
Notting Hill Carnival, *Iconic London* celebrates a city of
colourful contrasts and unique character.

Published by VisitBritain in association with
Visit London, this beautiful collection of photographs
provides a fascinating insight into the life of one
of the world's great capitals. *Iconic London* also includes
a gazetteer of visitor information and contact details
for many of the places and destinations featured.

p8-13 The Houses of Parliament on the site of the Palace of Westminster, a former royal palace and residence of kings

13

p14 & 15 Number 10 Downing Street, the historic
office and home of the British Prime Minister

p16-19 Changing the Guard at Buckingham Palace

That monarch of the road,
Observer of the Highway Code,
That big-six wheeler
Scarlet-painted
London Transport
Diesel-engined
Ninety-seven horse power Omnibus!

MICHAEL FLANDERS AND DONALD SWANN

All the world's a stage,
And all the men and women merely players:
They have their exits and their entrances;
And one man in his time plays many parts.

WILLIAM SHAKESPEARE

AGATHA CHRI

'EVEN MORE
THRILLING THAN THE
PLOT IS THE
ATMOSPHERE OF
SHUDDERING

THE PETER SAUNDERS PRESENTS

the Mousetrap

TIE'S THE MOUSETRAP

p28 Shakespeare's Globe, a reconstruction of the open-air theatre where his plays were originally performed
p30-31 Agatha Christie's The Mousetrap, London theatre's longest running show
p32-33 The bright lights of Piccadilly Circus

*So come with me, where dreams
are born, and time is never planned.
Just think of happy things, and your
heart will fly on wings, forever, in
Never Never Land!*

J.M. BARRIE

p34–35 The underwater world of the London Aquarium
p36 Statue of Peter Pan in Kensington Gardens, Hyde Park
p38 & 39 Runners at the annual London Marathon

Poetry and Dream

2

Surrealism and Beyond

For the poets and artists of the Surrealist movement, dreams stood for all aspects of the world repressed by rationalism and convention.

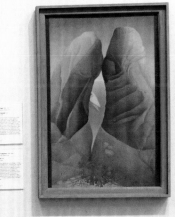

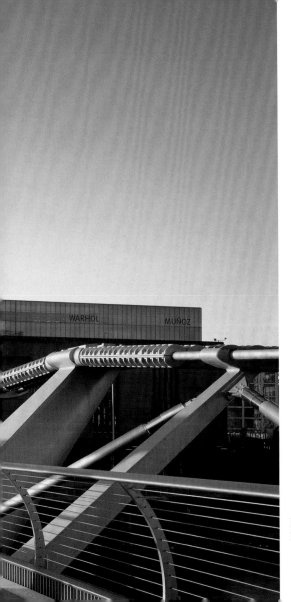

WARHOL   MUÑOZ

p40-41 Paintings in the Tate Modern collection
p42-43 The Millennium Bridge leading to Tate Modern

Thou stately stream
that with the swelling tide
'Gainst London walls
incessantly dost beat,
Thou Thames, I say, where
barge and boat doth ride.

GEORGE TURBERVILLE

49

p50-51 Festive Christmas lights in Regent Street
p52-53 Harrods at night, lit by over 11,000
energy-efficient light bulbs

Her cutty-sark, o' Paisley harn
That while a lassie she had worn,
In longitude tho' sorely scanty,
It was her best, and she was vauntie

[Her short underskirt, o' Paisley cloth,
That while a young lass she had
worn,
In longitude though very limited,
It was her best, and she was proud]
ROBERT BURNS

57

p60 & 61 Trendy Carnaby Street in London's West End

p62-63 Chinese New Year celebrations in Trafalgar Square
p64 & 65 Colourful Notting Hill Carnival, Europe's largest street festival

THE GAP

p66-67 'Mind the Gap' on a London Underground platform
p68 Stunning entrance of Canary Wharf Underground station
p69 Canada Water Underground sign

Architecture aims at eternity.

SIR CHRISTOPHER WREN

p71~73 St Paul's Cathedral, designed by Sir Christopher Wren

p74-75 Seasonal ice skating on the frozen courtyard
of Somerset House
p76-77 British Airways London Eye in the snow
p78-79 Skateboarder performing an 'ollie' in front
of the London Eye

And let thy feet, millenniums hence
be set in midst of knowledge.

ALFRED LORD TENNYSON

and let thy feet
millenniums hence
be set in midst of knowledge

p81 The soaring Great Court of the British Museum
p82 Museum of London, telling the story of London past and present
p83 The British Library's imposing entrance and courtyard

*Dinosaurs
are nature's
special effects.*

ROBERT T. BAKKER

85

89

This City now doth
like a garment wear
The beauty of the
morning; silent, bare,
Ships, towers, domes,
theatres, and temples lie
Open unto the fields,
and to the sky;
All bright and glittering
in the smokeless air.

WILLIAM WORDSWORTH

91

97

*Three hundred years ago
a prisoner condemned
to the Tower of London
carved on the wall of his
cell this sentiment to keep
up his spirits during his
long imprisonment:
'It is not adversity that
kills, but the impatience
with which we bear adversity'.*

FATHER JAMES KELLER

p98~99 Aerial view of the Tower of London
p100 Yeoman Warder, Tower of London
p101 Traitor's Gate, Tower of London

p102~103 Secret Intelligence Service Headquarters
on the Thames, commonly known as the MI6 Building
p104 & 105 City of London: new buildings including the Swiss Re
Building (affectionately known as the Gherkin) and street sign

Westminster Abbey is nature crystallized into a conventional form by man, with his sorrows, his joys, his failures, and his seeking for the Great Spirit. It is a frozen requiem, with a nation's prayer ever in dumb music ascending.

M.E.W. SHERWOOD

p106~109 Westminster Abbey, scene of the coronation,
marriage and burial of British monarchs
p110 & 111 Trafalgar Square: the National Gallery and fountain;
statue of Admiral Lord Nelson on top of Nelson's Column

111

p112~113 Royal Albert Hall, venue for the traditional Proms concerts
p114~115 A smiling Chelsea Pensioner at the annual Chelsea Flower Show

Gazetteer

British Airways London Eye (p76-79)
Riverside Building, County Hall, Westminster Bridge Road, SE1 7PB
T: 0870 500 0600   W: ba-londoneye.com
Since it opened in 2000, British Airways London Eye has become a symbol of London and is recognised worldwide. At 135m, it is the world's tallest observation wheel, giving panoramic views of up to 40km.

British Library (p83)
96 Euston Road, NW1 2DB
T: 020 7412 7222   W: bl.uk
The British Library is a treasure house of books, manuscripts, maps, stamps and sound recordings. It has galleries, a public events programme, bookshop and guided tours. Reading rooms accessible by reader's pass only.

British Museum (p81)
Great Russell Street, WC1B 3DG
T: 020 7323 8299   W: thebritishmuseum.ac.uk
Permanent display and special exhibitions of works of man from prehistory to the present day. Permanent displays of antiquities from around the world.

Buckingham Palace (p16-19)
SW1A 1AA
T: 020 7766 7300   W: royalcollection.org.uk
Buckingham Palace is the official London residence of The Queen and serves as both home and office. Its 19 state rooms form the heart of the palace and are lavishly furnished with some of the finest treasures from the Royal Collection.

Chelsea Physic Garden (p114-115)
66 Royal Hospital Road, SW3 4HS
T: 020 7376 3910   W: chelseaphysicgarden.co.uk
The garden was founded in 1673 and continues today as a haven for medicinal and rare plants.

Cutty Sark Clipper Ship (p56-57)
King William Walk, Greenwich, SE10 9HT
T: 020 8858 3445   W: cuttysark.org.uk
The last and most famous tea-clipper. Explore every part of the ship including the Lower Hold with its collection of figure-heads, and the Tween Deck, which tells the story of the Cutty Sark and has a display of ship pictures and models.

Houses of Parliament Public Galleries (p8-13)
Westminster, SW1A 0AA
T: 020 7219 4272   W: parliament.uk
This is a working institution. It is in a superb building by Barry and Pugin with medieval survival, (Westminster Hall).

Hyde Park (p94-95)
T: 020 7262 5484   W: royalparks.gov.uk
Hyde Park is famous for boating and swimming in its lake, The Serpentine, and its riding track, Rotten Row, the first public road to be lit at night.

Kensington Gardens (p36)
T: 020 7262 5484   W: royalparks.gov.uk
Kensington Gardens were originally formed in 1689 with land from Hyde Park when William and Mary moved into Nottingham House, now Kensington Palace.

London Aquarium (p34-35)

County Hall, Riverside Building, SE1 7PB
T: 020 7967 8000   W: londonaquarium.co.uk
Over 350 species from every major environment across the globe, plus daily talks, dives and feeds.

Museum of London (p82)

150 London Wall, EC2Y 5HN
T: 0870 444 3852   W: museumoflondon.org.uk
The Museum of London is the world's largest urban history museum, the permanent galleries tell the story of London from pre-historic times to the present.

National Gallery (p110-111)

Trafalgar Square, WC2N 5DN
T: 020 7747 2888   W: nationalgallery.org.uk
The National Gallery has one of the greatest collections of European paintings in the world. A permanent collection spans the period 1250 - 1900 and consists of over 2,300 Western European paintings by many of the world's famous artists.

Natural History Museum (p84-85)

Cromwell Road, SW7 5BD
T: 020 7942 5000   W: nhm.ac.uk
The Natural History Museum reveals how the jigsaw of life fits together. Animal, vegetable or mineral, the best of our planet's most amazing treasures are here.

Old Royal Naval College (p54-55)

Cutty Sark Gardens, Greenwich, SE10 9LW
T: 020 8269 4791   W: greenwichfoundation.org.uk
The Old Royal Naval College, in the heart of Maritime Greenwich, is the site of the Greenwich Royal Hospital for Seamen, built to the designs of Sir Christopher Wren, which later became the Royal Naval College.

Portobello Road Market (p45)

Portobello Road, 72 Tavistock Road, W11 1AN
T: 020 7727 7684
Antiques (Saturdays), clothes, accessories, second hand goods (Friday and Saturdays), fruit and vegetables, CDs.

Queen's House (p54-55)

Romney Road, Greenwich, SE10 9NF
T: 020 8858 4422   W: nmm.ac.uk
The first Palladian-style house in England (1635) designed by Inigo Jones for the Stuart queens Anne of Denmark and Henrietta Maria. Elegant interiors provide the setting for displays of portraits / paintings of Greenwich and naval history.

Royal Albert Hall (p112-113)

Kensington Gore, SW7 2AP
T: 020 7589 8212   W: royalalberthall.com
Internationally renowned venue offering visitors a wide variety of entertainment - classical music, rock and pop, jazz, sporting events, galas, banquets and balls. Open during the day for tours of the building.

Science Museum (p86-87)

Exhibition Road, SW7 2DD
T: 0870 870 4868   W: sciencemuseum.org.uk
The Science Museum offers an IMAX cinema, simulators, special exhibitions and amazing permanent collections. It's a great destination for anyone of all ages looking for an exciting excursion.

Shakespeare's Globe Exhibition and Tour (p28)

New Globe Walk, Bankside, SE1 9DT

T: 020 7902 1500   W: shakespeares-globe.org

Shakespeare's Globe Exhibition and Theatre Tour offer a fascinating introduction to the Globe Theatre and life in Shakespeare's London.

Somerset House (p74-75)

Strand, WC2R 1LA

T: 020 7845 4670   W: somerset-house.org.uk

Somerset House is a place for enjoyment, refreshment, arts and learning. This magnificent 18thC building houses the celebrated collections of the Courtauld Institute of Art Gallery, Gilbert Collection and Hermitage Rooms.

St James's Park (p92-93)

T: 020 7930 1793

St James's Park is a very popular park with tourists and workers alike. It is famous for its views, waterfowl and flower displays.

St Paul's Cathedral (p71-73)

St Paul's Churchyard, EC4M 8AD

T: 020 7246 8357   W: stpauls.co.uk

A Cathedral dedicated to St Paul has overlooked the City of London since 640AD. The current Cathedral was designed by Sir Christopher Wren and built between 1675 and 1710 after its predecessor was destroyed in the Great Fire of London.

Tate Modern (p40-41)

Bankside, SE1 9TG

T: 020 7887 8008   W: tate.org.uk

Tate Modern is the UK's largest modern art gallery presenting masterpieces by Dali, Picasso, Warhol and Matisse. Visit the art collections for free or catch one of the exhibitions that are presented throughout the year.

Tower Bridge Exhibition (p58-59)

Tower Bridge, SE1 2UP

T: 020 7403 3761   W: towerbridge.org.uk

Inside Tower Bridge Exhibition you will travel up to the high-level walkways, located 140 feet above the Thames and witness stunning panoramic views of London before visiting the Victorian Engine Rooms. See the original machinery in action.

Tower of London (p98-101)

Tower Hill, EC3N 4AB

T: 0870 756 6060   W: hrp.org.uk

The Tower of London spans over 900 years of British history. Fortress, palace, prison, arsenal and garrison, it is one of the most famous fortified buildings in the world, and houses the Crown Jewels, armouries, Yeoman Warders and ravens.

Victoria and Albert Museum (p88-89)

Cromwell Road, SW7 2RL

T: 020 7942 2000   W: vam.ac.uk

One of the world's leading museums of art and design and home to 3,000 years' worth of amazing artefacts from many of the world's richest cultures.

Westminster Abbey (p106-109)

Parliament Square, SW1P 3PA

T: 020 7222 5152   W: westminster-abbey.org

One of Britain's finest Gothic buildings. Scene of the coronation, marriage and burial of British monarchs. Nave and cloisters, Royal Chapels and Undercroft Museum.

Image acknowledgements

Actionplus Sports	3
Bosworth, Daniel	78
britainonview.com	8, 28, 30, 36, 71, 76, 92, 98, 106, 108, 111
de Witt, Kathy	82, 105
Dublin, Sheradon	10, 96
FCO/Fabijanic, Damir	68, 81, 104, 110,
Holt, Andrew	34, 46, 72, 84, 102
imagesource.com	4
Knight, Martin	26
Libera, Pawel	15, 16, 18, 19, 23, 50, 101
Lichfield	65
McCormick-McAdam	32, 56, 90
McKinlay, Doug	12, 20
Nathan, Eric	24, 52, 69
Noton, David	58
Pritchard, Grant	39, 62
Rasmussen, Ingrid	44, 45
Rogues-Rogery, Olivier	3, 100
Sellman, David	42
Spaull, Jon	64
Teer, Jasmine	front cover, 74, 94, 112
TNT Magazine	66
Troika/Walter, Michael	114
Visit London	14, 40, 48, 54, 83, 86, 88
White, Juliet	60, 61

All the photographs featured in *Iconic London* are supplied by britainonview.com, the official online image library of VisitBritain.

Britainonview

Quotation acknowledgements

22   Michael Flanders (1922-1975) and Donald Swann (1923-1994), A Transport of Delight (The Omnibus). Words by Michael Flanders and Music by Donald Swann © Flanders and Swann. All rights administered by Warner/Chapell Music Ltd, London W6 8BS. Reproduced by permission.

29   William Shakespeare (1564-1616), *As You Like It* (1599) act 2, sc. 7, 1.139

37   James Matthew Barrie (1860-1937), *Peter Pan* (2007), Penguin Books Ltd

47   George Turberville (c1540-c1597), source unconfirmed

57   Robert Burns (1759-1796), *Tam O'Shanter* (1791)

70   Sir Christopher Wren (1632-1723), source unconfirmed

80   Alfred Lord Tennyson (1809-1892), *The Two Voices* (1832)

91   William Wordsworth (1770-1850), *Composed upon Westminster Bridge* (1807)

99   Father James Keller (1900-1977), source unconfirmed

107   Mary Elizabeth Wilson Sherwood (1826-1903), source unconfirmed